FAMOUS FAMILIES™

MUHAMMAD ALI
AND
LAILA ALI

TIM UNGS

The Rosen Publishing Group, Inc., New York

Published in 2005 by The Rosen Publishing Group, Inc.
29 East 21st Street, New York, NY 10010

First Edition

Library of Congress Cataloging-in-Publication Data
Tim Ungs.
Muhammad Ali and Laila Ali / Tim Ungs.—1st ed.
 p. cm.—(Famous families)
Includes bibliographical references and index.
ISBN 1-4042-0261-7 (library binding)
1. Ali, Muhammad, 1942– —Juvenile literature. 2. Ali, Laila—Juvenile literature.
3. Boxers (Sports)—United States—Biography—Juvenile literature. 4. Women boxers—United States—Biography—Juvenile literature.
I. Title. II. Series.
GV1131.K46 2005
796.83'092'2—dc22

2004013390

Manufactured in the United States of America

Contents

BREAKING THE NEWS TO DAD

January 1999. Los Angeles. She was nervous, but she knew she couldn't keep him in the dark any longer. As Laila Ali recounts in her autobiography, *Reach*, she had been waiting for the right time to tell her father about her decision. Now he was in town. She walked into his hotel suite, kissed him on the cheek, and got to the point. "I need to talk to you about something," she said. "I know you've been hearing talk about me boxing. Well, it's true. I didn't want to tell you until I was sure."

It would be hard for any daughter to tell her father she was going to hit and be hit for a living. It was that much harder for Laila Ali because of who her father is. He is Muhammad Ali, three-time heavy-weight boxing champion. In January 1999, when this conversation took place, his hands trembled and his speech was painfully slow. The tremors and speech problems were both symptoms of Parkinson's syndrome, a tragic disease many say was made worse by all the years of punishment he took in the boxing ring.

Pictured here in 1977 with his newborn daughter, Laila, Muhammad Ali shows a different side from the one that made him one of the most successful boxing champions in history. Laila is Ali's sixth child and fifth daughter. *(Inset)* Twenty-one years later, Ali watches Laila's boxing debut, which she won by knockout in thirty-one seconds.

On hearing news like this, any father would be concerned for his daughter's safety. Any father who had firsthand experience of the horrors of boxing would be worried sick. Boxing takes its toll on all who put on the gloves. Not even a champion avoids punishment.

Muhammad Ali had a professional career that spanned more than sixty bouts. He traded shots with such bruising hitters as George Foreman and Joe Frazier, and he paid a great physical price for his glory. As Laila recounts in *Reach*, Ali gave voice to his misgivings about his daughter's career choice. "Being a fighter ain't easy," he declared. "What are you going to do when you get hit upside your head, get all dizzy, and don't know where you are?"

While Laila's announcement was indeed upsetting, Muhammad Ali knew two things. He knew his daughter was the kind of girl who could take care of herself. He also knew she would never accept being told what to do. In both respects, she bore more than a passing resemblance to her father. "Dad never listened to anybody," she told a reporter for the *New York Times*, "so what can he say?"

The bond between father and daughter was strong, even though they had basically lived separate lives since Laila was a young girl.

Laila and her sister Hana are the only children of Ali and Veronica Porche. (The two girls have eight stepsiblings from their father's other marriages.) At the height of Ali's fame, in the early 1970s, the family lived together in Los Angeles. But Ali and Veronica divorced when Laila was seven, and Ali moved to a farm in Michigan. Laila saw him only on summer vacations and on his occasional trips to Los Angeles.

It might seem that the daughter of Muhammad Ali would have an easy and enviable life, but Laila's has been a difficult journey. She rejected the comforts of glamorous Malibu, California, where her mother had moved after the divorce. Instead, she chose to travel by bus each day to go to school in the city of Los Angeles. "I was one of those kids who was trying to get into the ghetto when everyone else was trying to get out, because I wanted to experience the other side," she told the *New York Times.*

Laila switched schools often and made a number of bad decisions. She got into street fights, was arrested for shoplifting, and spent time in juvenile hall as well as a group home for girls. However, she learned from her humiliating experiences and saw that she needed to get her life together. As she made her revelation to her father, she could proudly claim to have a business degree from Santa Monica Community College. In addition, she had her own business—a thriving nail salon. And she was spending many hours each day training to become a professional boxer. She had still not thrown a punch in a competitive fight, but her ring debut was not far off.

Muhammad Ali thought about his daughter's words. He did not like what he heard. "No matter what you say, Laila, I'm still going to worry about you. You're my baby girl."

"I respect how you feel, Daddy, but I've made up my mind," she responded. To soften her harsh tone, she added, "I'll never do it in a way that brings dishonor to you or myself."

Muhammad Ali remained silent. Laila was determined, but she also desperately wanted her father's support. His face—frozen stiff by the effects of Parkinson's—gave no sign of how he felt. Try as she might, she could not read his expression.

At last, he spoke. "OK, come over here and show me your left jab."

 **CHAPTER 1**

THE KING OF THE WORLD

Muhammad Ali was born when the Second World War was still raging, and he grew up in the American South before the advent of the civil rights struggle. In Ali's youth, blacks had to settle for second-class status. It meant eating in separate, blacks-only restaurants. It meant sitting at the back of the bus. It meant threats if you strayed too far from your own neighborhood.

Beginnings

Born in Louisville, Kentucky, on January 17, 1942, Cassius Marcellus Clay (who would later be known as Muhammad Ali), was given the name of his father. The elder Cassius was himself named for a famous white abolitionist (an opponent of slavery in the period just before the Civil War). Young Cassius had a relatively stable upbringing. Many men who turn to boxing do so to escape poverty and abuse. Cassius's youth, while not one of luxury by any means, was pleasant in comparison to the childhoods of other champions, such as

In 1954, a thin twelve-year-old boy named Cassius Clay had just begun to study and practice the sport he would later redefine. Eleven years after this photograph was taken, Clay was well on his way to making boxing history.

Joe Frazier, Sonny Liston, or Floyd Patterson. Cassius's family was not rich, but both parents worked, and young Cassius had the kinds of favorite possessions any young boy might treasure. In fact, one of these possessions, a brand-new red bicycle, played a key role in leading to his first fateful encounter with his destiny.

It All Started with a Bicycle

The year was 1954. Twelve-year-old Cassius and a friend left their bikes outside the Columbia Auditorium and went inside to view the exhibits at the Louisville Home Show. When the boys came outside, they saw that Cassius's bicycle was gone. Cassius was heartsick and angry. Someone told him to report the crime to police officer Joe Martin. Martin, off-duty at the time, happened to be teaching boxing to kids in the basement of the auditorium. Young Cassius burst into the basement, ranting and raving, and told Martin how he was going to beat up whoever stole his bike. The policeman told him he'd better learn to fight first. Then, Martin suggested boxing lessons. Cassius liked the sound of that and soon became a constant visitor to Martin's gym. After his first, somewhat shaky, victory, the 89-pound (40 kilograms) Cassius shouted that he would soon be "the greatest of all time."

The young boxer, while inexperienced, showed promise. He had quick feet and hands, great reflexes, and the ability to think clearly, even after being hit. Above all, he had the desire and discipline to work harder than everyone else. "He was always the first in and last out of the gym," his trainer Angelo Dundee told *Time* magazine. Cassius's rise was steady and spectacular. He became national Golden Gloves champ. He won the boxing gold medal at the 1960 Olympics in Rome. He came back to

In 1960, Cassius Clay won the Olympic Gold Medal for light heavyweight boxing. Clay, at the time a shy, unknown eighteen-year-old, was so proud of his medal he kept it on for a full two days after his win.

the United States and recorded nineteen straight professional victories. By February 1964, he had earned a shot at the heavyweight crown.

"Gaseous Cassius" Takes the Stage

When he burst onto the scene, the world had never seen anything like Cassius Marcellus Clay. He was in Miami to fight Sonny Liston for the title. He was a seven-to-one underdog. Nobody thought he

Boxer . . . And Poet

Before every fight, Ali composed a humorous poem predicting how many rounds it would take for him to beat his opponent. For the first fight against Sonny Liston, he entertained reporters with this:

I predict that he will go in eight to prove that I'm great; and if he wants to go to heaven, I'll get him in seven. If you want to lose your money, bet on Sonny.

For what was perhaps his most famous fight, the 1971 bout versus Joe Frazier, he composed the following:

Joe's gonna come out smokin'
But I ain't gonna be jokin'
I'll be pickin' and pokin'
Pouring water on his smokin'
This might shock and amaze ya
But I'm gonna destroy Joe Frazier.

could win. Sportswriters literally feared for his life at the hands of his opponent. The hard-punching Liston was a tough character whose work history included collecting debts for loan sharks. Even Cassius's own handlers were worried. Before the fight, Cassius's doctor, Ferdie Pacheco, made a point of memorizing the quickest route to the local hospital.

Did young Cassius Clay act like someone about to get pummeled? Not exactly. Even though he was the challenger, he acted like the star of the show. He bragged, he boasted, and he acted crazy for the reporters. His bragging ways had already earned him such nicknames as the Louisville Lip and Gaseous Cassius. At the weigh-in on the morning of the fight, he proclaimed himself to be "the prettiest

Muhammad Ali was as famous for his endless self-promotion and bragging as he was for his boxing style and political activism. Pictured here, his trainer, Angelo Dundee, jokingly tries to silence the Louisville Lip before a 1963 fight against Doug Jones. Ali won the fight in ten rounds.

fighter in the world." He taunted Liston, calling the champ a "chump" and an "ugly old bear." "I'm gonna eat you alive!" he shouted. And for the first time, he and his sidekick Bundini Brown chanted the famous catchphrase "Float like a butterfly, sting like a bee." If he was scared, he wasn't acting like it. He was, however, acting like a lunatic.

On the evening of the fight, there were rumors that Cassius had gotten on a plane and fled. But, of course, he was right there in the

arena, quietly watching the preliminary bouts. Cassius's less talented brother Rudy was fighting and won a hard decision. As recounted in David Remnick's book, *King of the World*, Cassius assured his brother, "After tonight, Rudy, you won't have to fight no more."

Shocking the World

The main event: Cassius not only survived the first round, he won it easily. The younger fighter was the aggressor, which surprised the crowd, not to mention his opponent. Cassius was in complete control until the fourth round. By accident or design (to this day, no one knows), something from Liston's gloves got into Cassius's eyes. As the round ended, Cassius staggered back to his corner, shouting, "I'm blind," and told his trainer Angelo Dundee to cut his gloves off— meaning he was through fighting. But Dundee would have none of it. According to *King of the World*, he told his fighter, "This is the big one, daddy. . . . We're not quitting now. You go out there and you run."

Dundee rinsed Cassius's eyes and pushed him back into the ring. Cassius struggled through the fifth round, half blind, keeping Liston at bay with his superior reach. In the middle of the sixth round, he blinked his eyes clear and took control of the fight, landing punches at will. Liston, used to knocking out his opponents early, couldn't keep up with the younger, faster fighter. Cassius dominated the sixth round and went to his stool to rest for the seventh. Then, suddenly, as he told writer Alex Haley, "[He gave] a whoop and [came] off that stool like it was red hot." He had seen Liston spit out his mouthpiece. The champion was not answering the bell for the seventh. "I am the king. King of the world! Eat your words! Eat! Eat your words!" Cassius, the new heavyweight champion, shouted to all who had doubted him.

It would not be the last time he had to prove his critics wrong. Meanwhile, the public, while somewhat embarrassed by the thuggish Liston, was even less thrilled with the new champion. In 1964, boxers, especially black boxers, were meant to be seen and not heard. When they did speak, they were expected to be very polite. Cassius's bragging did not sit well with Middle America.

Cassius Becomes Muhammad

To make matters worse, the day after becoming champ, Cassius confirmed the rumor that he was a member of the Nation of Islam. He renounced his last name, which he said was a slave name. He said that from then on he

Muhammad Ali, then Cassius Clay, is shown here in the 1964 heavyweight championship match against Sonny Liston. Ali took the world champion title from Liston in seven rounds.

would be called Cassius X. Two weeks later, Elijah Muhammad, the leader of the Nation of Islam, gave him the name we all know him by, Muhammad Ali.

To say that Muhammad Ali was an unpopular champion at first is putting it mildly. He had trouble finding places to defend his title. His rematch with Liston was held at a boys' club in a small town in Maine because none of the major boxing venues would have anything to do with the fight. There were rumors circulating that

Here, Cassius Clay jokes with leading Nation of Islam figure Malcolm X, in a diner in Miami, Florida, after beating Sonny Liston in the ring. The next day, Clay would officially announce his membership in the Nation of Islam.

involved "hits" by the mob and/or the Nation of Islam. In a charged, high-security atmosphere, Liston was again favored to win. This time, he went down in the first round, felled by what many considered to be a "phantom punch." In one of the most famous sports photos of all time, Ali stood over Liston with his right arm cocked. He was shouting, "Get up and fight, you bum! . . . Nobody will believe this!"

Shown here in Toronto, Canada, in 1966, Ali rests up before his fight against George Chuvalo. Ali is pointing out a newspaper headline that shows that thousands of people share his stance against the Vietnam War.

No Quarrel with the Vietcong

Another fight, another controversy. Eight more successful title defenses followed. And then came the biggest controversy of all. In April 1967, Muhammad Ali refused to be drafted into the army. He felt that being in the military would conflict with his status as a preacher of Islam. "I ain't got no quarrel with those Vietcong anyway," he told reporters, referring to the Vietnamese armed forces that were fighting against the

United States. His words shocked America. At that time, opposition to the Vietnam conflict was not nearly as widespread as it would later become. Muhammad Ali's defiance did not seem like an act of principle. It simply seemed unpatriotic. This gave even more people reason to hate him. As a result of his stance, the boxing authorities stripped him of his title and he was barred from being able to make a living in the ring.

During the three and one-half years of his exile from boxing, Ali earned money by lecturing—mainly on college campuses. Over time, more and more people came to agree with Muhammad Ali's opposition to the war, and he began to be admired for it. "For all Ali knew, he'd never fight again, never see another big purse," wrote Bob Costas in an article in *Rolling Stone* magazine. "He risked it all for what he believed. Ultimately, this earned him the respect of even those who initially reviled [hated] him."

After nearly four years of legal proceedings, the U.S. Supreme Court overturned Ali's conviction for refusing to be drafted. Free to box again, Ali began his quest to win back his title. He faced Joe Frazier— the man who became his greatest rival—in New York's Madison Square Garden on March 8, 1971. The first of the three legendary Ali-Frazier meetings, it was a battle that lived up to its billing. Promoters simply called it The Fight. Ali lost a tough fifteen-round decision, but it was Frazier who spent three weeks in the hospital recovering.

The Rumble and the Thrilla

In October 1974, Ali traveled to Africa to fight George Foreman in what was promoted as the Rumble in the Jungle. (There, he began his relationship with Laila's mother, Veronica.) As with the Liston fight, the press feared for Ali's life, thinking him overmatched, but again Ali shocked the world. He won with one of the most brilliant tactical ploys ever used in sports. Instead of relying on mobility and speed, Ali triumphed because he was able to absorb punishment.

For much of the early rounds, he simply leaned back on the ropes (which, craftily, he insisted be looser than usual) and let the powerful Foreman tire himself out. Ali slipped a number of punches, but he took some mighty licks. The "Rope-a-dope," as he came to call it, was a surprise even to his trainers, who were screaming at him to get off the ropes. By the eighth round, Foreman had worn himself out. Having saved

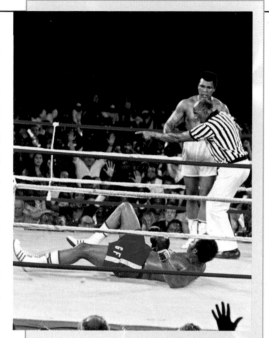

In this 1974 photo, the referee of the Rumble in the Jungle directs Ali to the corner while George Foreman lies stunned on the ground for a count of ten seconds. In accordance with boxing rules, the referee declared Ali the winner by knockout.

much of his energy while leaning on the ropes, Ali was able to spring into action. He showered Foreman with blows and knocked out the bigger, heavily favored fighter.

One year later, Ali met Joe Frazier, for the third and final time, in the Philippines. In what was called the Thrilla in Manila, Ali did little

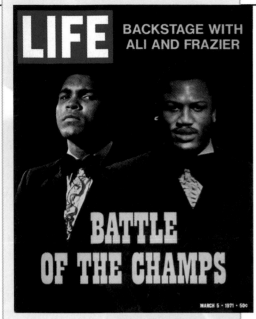

LIFE BACKSTAGE WITH ALI AND FRAZIER

BATTLE OF THE CHAMPS

MARCH 5 • 1971 • 50¢

Shown here is the cover of the March 6, 1971, issue of *Life* magazine, which covered the first boxing match between Ali and Joe Frazier. The fight, billed as the Fight of the Century, was held at New York City's Madison Square Garden on March 8, 1971.

dancing and a lot of hitting. As he had done in the Foreman fight, he relied on his ability to take punishment, and Frazier was more than willing to dole it out. Ringside observers agreed that this was one of the greatest boxing competitions of all time. For fourteen rounds, the two brave boxers hammered each other. As the bell for the final round rang, Frazier, his left eye completely swollen shut, was held down on his stool by his trainer, Eddie Futch. At almost the same time, Ali collapsed to the floor in his corner. Later, as recounted in Thomas Hauser's book *Muhammad Ali: His Life and Times*, Ali acknowledged, "Frazier quit just before I did."

The Later Years: Taking a Beating

Ali's boxing career did not end with the Thrilla in Manila, but it should have. He went on to fight ten more times. He lost and regained the title again, but at great cost. Why did he keep fighting? Was it for pride? For vanity? The desire or need for money? No one knows, but it was not in Ali's best interests to continue boxing until he was nearly forty. As a highly intelligent boxer, he realized that what had carried him through his glory years—speed, reach, reflexes—were the attributes of a young boxer. He couldn't count on them to be an advantage forever.

Ali's later success depended on raw courage and the ability to absorb blows. His final title fight, which was against his former sparring partner Larry Holmes, was a disgrace from start to finish. It brought shame to the promoters of the fight and to the boxing establishment that allowed it to happen. Perhaps Ali had shocked the world too many times, because sportswriters gave him a good chance to win against Holmes. However, the truth was that he could have been killed in the ring that night. It was "the worst sports event I ever had to cover," wrote *Washington Post* journalist Dave Kindred. "Ali had that great fighter's heart, boundless courage, all that pride. It was like watching an automobile accident that kills someone you love. Round after round, he kept going out. And if they'd let him, he would have gone out for more."

The final five years of Ali's career are a chilling demonstration of what boxing can do to even the greatest fighter. It's likely that boxing historians of the future will remember Ali at the height of his powers, and rightly so. The best summation of Ali's career might come from his greatest opponent, Joe Frazier, who, after the Thrilla in Manilla, said, "We were gladiators . . . I don't like him but I got to say, in the ring he was a man. In Manila, I hit him punches, those punches, they'd of knocked a building down. And he took 'em. He took 'em and he came back, and I got to respect that part of the man."

CHAPTER 2

"THE BLOOD OF A CHAMPION RUNS THROUGH MY VEINS"

Because she was born at the end of Muhammad Ali's fabled career, Laila never had the chance to see her father fight. In fact, she first learned about his career when, as she writes in her autobiography, *Reach*, "I had to write book reports for school and, out of laziness, chose him as my subject."

Closer to her mother, Veronica Porche, than to her famous dad, Laila had to make her own way in the world. "My parents, for all their wonderful qualities, didn't give me a lot of guidance. The guidance I found was hidden deep inside. I saw that guidance when I started taking responsibility for myself—and owning my own story," she writes in *Reach*. After a number of false starts (including a couple of scrapes with the law), Laila's life was beginning to come together when she saw what would become her destiny. On St. Patrick's Day, 1996, Laila, then eighteen years old,

Laila Ali, Muhammad Ali's youngest daughter, poses here for a publicity shot at a large bookstore in New York City in 2001. As glamorous as always, Laila appeared at several bookstores to sign copies of *Reach*, her autobiography.

was hanging out at a friend's house. The television was tuned to the Mike Tyson-Frank Bruno fight. Two women, Christy Martin and Deirdre Gogarty, were featured in a preliminary bout. It was a hard-fought, thrilling contest, and it played a large part in putting women's boxing on the map. Laila experienced what she would later recall as "a revelation" at that very moment.

As she recounts in *Reach*, she said, "I can do this," to her friend, Alice.

"Do what?" [replied Alice].

"Be a fighter," [Laila responded].

"Are you serious?"

"Yes."

"You're crazy, Laila," said Alice's dad. "You're not the kind of girl who belongs in the ring. These women are rough. They'd love to whup a pretty girl like you."

"No one's gonna whup me."

Training for Glory

The seed was planted. Laila added tough workouts to her already busy routine of running a nail salon and going to school. She saw her father occasionally, but she never brought up the subject of boxing. As fate would have it, she met the man who would shape her life and boxing destiny at a celebration for her father's fifty-seventh birthday in Las Vegas in 1999. The man, Yahya McClain, was himself a former champion boxer. At first, Laila was put off by McClain's extreme confidence and by his obvious interest in her. As she writes in *Reach*, she even heard him tell her father, "I'm going to marry her." Laila couldn't believe his nerve. But she gave him her phone number anyway.

Back in Los Angeles, Laila and Yahya agreed to meet for coffee. They began to click—both as a couple and as a team. Yahya took charge of Laila's development as a boxer, even to the point of enforcing a strict diet. He matched Laila up with trainer Dub Huntley, and her talents blossomed.

Laila's professional career began in October 1999. Fighting as a 165-pound (75 kg) super-middleweight, Laila had no trouble with her first opponent, April Fowler. The first professional victory for Ali's daughter was a knockout. Fowler lasted a little more than thirty seconds.

A greater struggle came with the press, which was critical of the fact that Fowler was a waitress and no match for Laila. But Yahya and Laila wanted to start with opponents who were somewhat inexperienced. She too had a day job. The Ali name would reveal itself to be both a blessing and a curse. It opened doors and raised expectations at the same time. Laila knew it wasn't entirely fair that because of who her father was, she would get $35,000 for a fight whereas most women boxers struggled by on much less. Because of this, she took the scrutiny of the press in stride.

The wins kept coming. Most of them were easy victories. One exception was an encounter with Karen Bill in Detroit, Michigan. With her father in attendance, Laila got knocked down by Bill, who was much bigger. Embarrassed and angered, Laila got up from the canvas and forgot the science of boxing—she simply pummeled her opponent. The fight ended in a third round TKO, or technical knockout. As she later recalls in *Reach*, Laila had a chat with her father after the fight. Concerned but supportive, the older Ali asked, "Were you worried when she knocked you down?"

"Not really," [replied Laila]. "You saw how I put it on her."

"Girl, you bad."

The Daughters Battle

On March 2, 2001, near the thirty-year anniversary of The Fight between Muhammad Ali and Joe Frazier, the boxers' daughters fought on the same card—meaning they fought on the same night, but not against each other. Jacqui Frazier-Lyde was thirty-eight, a lawyer and the mother of three children. She had come to boxing late but made up for her lack of skills with her wholehearted promotion of the upcoming bout. Frazier-Lyde was old enough to remember the great Ali-Frazier fights. She took the initiative in bringing about the matchup.

In promoting their fight, the two women switched the roles of their fathers. Jacqui took Ali's showman's approach to the contest. In contrast, Laila, who by this point had become the super-middleweight champion, was quiet and tight-lipped, not unlike Joe Frazier. The reversed dynamic made for good theater. Jacqui and Laila (who had adopted the nickname of She Bee Stingin) posed for the cover of magazines and appeared on the *Today* show together. But the boxing press sneered—as did the more established female boxers, such as Christy Martin. Martin complained to the *New York Times*, "You should have to pay your dues before you are in the spotlight like that." In response to such criticism, Laila wisely pointed out that the fight would bring women's boxing to the next level. "A lot of these girls don't realize that I'm in their corner," she told the *Times*. "They can be mad because I get all the attention, but I'm trying to help."

On June 8, 2001, Jacqui and Laila fought each other. It was perhaps the biggest night for women's boxing ever. Novelist Katherine Dunn, who was covering the event for *Sports Illustrated Women*, wrote, "It wasn't pretty. It wasn't finely skilled by any stretch. It was that scary, gorgeous thing that the ritualized crisis of boxing occasionally spawns—a real fight." Once-skeptical mainstream boxing figures like Lou Duva were impressed: "Nobody shoulda lost that fight! They both fought their hearts out! Boxing won!" Laila was the split-decision winner.

Laila lands a right hook on Jacqui Frazier-Lyde during their June 8, 2001, match in Verona, New York. Laila won the match in the eighth round by majority decision.

Alone at the Top

Laila has continued to blaze new ground since that fight. She holds three belts (or titles) at once. As well, she is the Super Middleweight Champ of three different boxing federations. In August 2003, she went up against Christy Martin, the woman who had originally inspired her to take up boxing. It was no match. Martin was still six inches shorter, at least twenty pounds lighter, and ten years older than Laila. She was at the tail end of her career, while Laila's was just getting into gear. Nevertheless, it was a good show for women's boxing. More important, it demonstrated that Laila had indeed come to the top of her profession.

CHAPTER 3

THIS IS MY CHILD

For the most part, Laila Ali grew up apart from her father, but she has fond memories of her early childhood, when the family was still together. As she would later write in *Reach* about her father, "He'd rescue, protect, and spoil us in any way he could." But there were tensions as well. Laila noticed the difference between her father's public personality and the private one. As she said, "I'd seen him leave waitresses hundred-dollar tips. I'd also seen him get distracted and forget us, actually leave the restaurant and have to return to fetch us kids." Laila also resisted her father's attempts at turning her into an obedient Muslim woman. She respected his religion but found it hard to endure the daily prayer rituals he forced her to perform. However, through good times and bad, she continued to love and respect her father.

Laila recalls in *Reach* that when she was a young woman, her father made comments about her wearing tight jeans and tank tops. "No Muslim daughter of mine should be running around in clothes that tight," he once told her. "I'd have to

Laila, heir to both of her parents' good looks as well as her father's toughness and her mother's grace, is pictured here in 1999, three months before her first professional fight.

remind him," she writes, "that for all the respect I gave his religion, it wasn't my religion . . . The discussions would break off before they got ugly. I'd firmly stand my ground until Dad would shake his head and say, 'You can't tell Laila anything. She's just like me.'"

After Muhammad and Laila's mother, Veronica, divorced in 1984, Laila continued to live with her mother and her sister Hana in Los Angeles. Ali moved to a farm in Michigan with his new wife Lonnie. Laila enjoyed going there to visit on summer vacations. One summer, she even took a job at a local McDonald's so she could be close to her father. As she writes in *Reach*, "Some people thought it was crazy for Ali's daughter to work in a fast-food restaurant, but I didn't care what they thought." Her father supported her decision, and in fact often visited Laila at work. He used Laila's job "as an excuse to drop by for apple pie and ice cream."

In the mid-1980s, Ali's health began to get worse. He had been diagnosed with Parkinson's syndrome, a chronic disease whose symptoms include trembling of the arms, jaw, legs, and face, as well as stiffness and slowness of movement. While he lost no mental sharpness, it became difficult for Ali to speak. To this day, he denies that his boxing career had anything to do with his Parkinson's, but many medical authorities disagree. As reported in *Muhammad Ali and His Times*, Dr. Dennis Cope (a prominent doctor who examined Ali regularly) put it bluntly, "If Muhammad hadn't been a professional fighter, none of these problems would have occurred."

While Laila remains unconvinced of the connection between her father's health problems and his boxing career, she has her own plans for avoiding excessive punishment in the ring. "My father had a whole different strategy," she told the *New York Times*. "He trained

Muhammad Ali is shown here at the Hollywood premiere of *Ali*, with his daughters Laila *(right)* and Hana *(left)*. In *Ali,* Will Smith plays the boxing legend. Smith had to gain 35 pounds (15.9 kg) for his role.

himself to be beat by opponents that were stronger than him. He took a lot more beatings than I plan on taking. And he fought a lot longer than I plan on fighting. I don't plan on taking much of a beating at all. I am a woman, and I want to give birth one day."

A Supportive and Loving Father

While Ali initially had reservations about Laila's boxing career, he overcame them. He has become more and more supportive and now regularly shows up at Laila's fights to cheer her on. The two have become a very media-friendly team. A few years ago, father and

Like Father, Like Daughter

Laila sees many similarities between herself and her father. "Me and my dad are so much alike that it keeps us from getting close. We both have very hard heads, and we do what we want to do," she writes in *Reach*. The Web site askmen.com quoted her at length on the subject: "Sometimes people can just be around me long enough to hear me hold a conversation and I'll remind them of my father. Sometimes people see me and they think I look like my father. And then, of course, when I get in the ring, it's very reminiscent of when my father fought, because we have the same build and body make-up, except I'm a female so there are some differences. But if you really study his old pictures, how he was built, [you'd notice] we are built the same way. We move a lot alike."

daughter teamed up for a "Got Milk?" promotion. More recently, they have been brought together by an ad campaign for Adidas sporting goods. The campaign's theme is "Impossible is nothing," and through modern film and video editing techniques, the advertisement's producers have indeed captured the impossible. The ad features Laila sparring with Ali in his prime. Laila is the aggressor and is trying hard to land a blow on her father. Ali successfully dances away from her jabs. At last, she gets a good punch in and knocks her father back. He shows surprise at being hit, then, leaning back against the ropes, winks and smiles at his daughter, more proud than hurt.

Ali and Laila appeared together in a number of promotional appearances for the "Impossible is nothing" ads. Because of his Parkinson's, the older Ali cannot always say much at these events, but he thrills the crowd with silent gestures and by his very presence. His daughter notices the adoration of her father's fans. "I grew up with my dad being the 'Greatest of All Time,'" she told the *New York Post*, "the most famous man in the world, so I'm very used to it . . . Kids need to see people who are great at what they do other than the celebrities and the rappers with all their ice [jewelry] on. They need to see some athletes, who work hard and strive to get better, so they can strive to do the same thing."

To one reporter for the *Journal News Online*, Laila expressed the hope that Muhammad Ali's fans would remember her father for the right reasons. "Kids look to anybody doing good, winning and making money. At the same time there's more to life than that. You still have to be a good human being, like my father. He's a humanitarian. He stood up for what he believed in, and he did what he wanted to inside and outside the ring."

Laila has continued her father's commitment to social issues. Here she teams up with Ali to give boxing lessons at a youth sports center in Harlem, in New York City.

CHAPTER 4

THE LEGACY

Laila, holder of three super-middleweight titles, looks to be the most likely person to bring women's boxing to a higher level of acceptance. Her victory over Christy Martin left her alone at the top of the boxing world. She now has eighteen wins and no losses. Fifteen of those wins came by knockout. As of this writing, a rematch looms with Jacqui Frazier-Lyde as well as a bout with tough contender Ann Wolfe. Some people think the Ali-Wolfe fight will be the biggest fight in women's boxing history. Laila Ali has already been featured in a few of those, and it seems certain she will be in many more.

The Champ: No Slowing Down

Muhammad Ali shows no signs of slowing down. For his boxing, he has been honored with numerous honors, such as *Sports Illustrated*'s "Athlete of the Century," the BBC's [British Broadcasting Corporation] "Sports Personality of the Century," the World Sports Award's "World Sportsman of the Century," and *GQ* magazine's "Athlete of the Century." However, he considers his postboxing humanitarian work to be even

Here, Laila takes a hit from Christy Martin during their 2003 match in Biloxi, Mississippi. Laila won the match when she knocked out Martin in the fourth round.

In this 1996 photograph, which captures a solemn moment, Muhammad Ali holds the Olympic torch before lighting the Olympic flame in Atlanta, Georgia.

more important. Ali once told Thomas Hauser, "I'm just getting started. All of my boxing, all of my running around, all of my publicity was just the start of my life. Now my life is really starting. Fighting injustice, fighting racism, fighting crime, fighting illiteracy, fighting poverty, using this face the world knows so well, and going out and fighting for truth and different causes."

The years immediately after his boxing career were quiet ones. Ali came back into the spotlight when he lit the ceremonial torch at the 1996 Olympic Games in Atlanta, Georgia. For millions of viewers, it was the first time they had seen Ali suffering the effects of Parkinson's. Many were moved to tears by his courage. Since the Atlanta Olympics, Ali's life has become a whirlwind of travel and promotion for charitable causes. He is on the road more than 300 days per year, an amazing figure for a man in his sixties suffering from Parkinson's disease. The Parkinson's, far from being a handicap, serves as a motivating force. As his wife, Lonnie, told *People* magazine, "Muhammad knows he has this illness for a reason. It's not by chance. Parkinson's disease has made him a more spiritual person. Muhammad believes God gave it to him to bring him to another level, to create another destiny."

For all he achieved in the ring, Muhammad Ali's postboxing achievements are perhaps more impressive. He has raised money for many causes, from the United Nations to the Special Olympics to the Make-A-Wish Foundation. He has negotiated hostage releases with Iraq and taken medical supplies to Cuba. He has brought 10 million meals to children in war-torn Liberia and led humanitarian missions to Afghanistan. In September 2000, he was named a United Nations Messenger of Peace. In May 2002, Lonnie and Muhammad testified before Congress on the state of Parkinson's research. In August 2002, the U.S. Senate passed the Muhammad Ali Boxing Reform Act. Among other things, this act protects boxers from coercive contracts and other exploitative business practices. In a meeting of two of the most beloved men in the world, he and the Dalai Lama were honored at the Tibetan Cultural Center in Bloomington, Indiana, in September 2003.

A major focus of Ali's energy is the building of the Muhammad Ali Center for the Advancement of Humanity in his hometown of Louisville. According to promotional literature from http://www.alicenter.org, the Ali Center will "serve as a place to celebrate the deeply rooted values and worldwide influence of Ali. Essentially, it will be a place that redeems and esteems the core values behind Ali himself—peace, social responsibility, respect and personal growth." Although there have been delays in the center's construction, plans as of this writing have it opening in spring 2005.

All of that would seem to be enough to occupy any man in his sixties, let alone one with Parkinson's. For all his achievements, he has one unfulfilled goal. "And one more thing," he told Thomas Hauser. "I'm still gonna find out who stole my bike when I was twelve years old in Louisville, and I'm still gonna whup him. That was a good bike."

TIMELINE

1942	• January 17, Cassius Marcellus Clay is born in Louisville, Kentucky.
1954	• Cassius's bicycle is stolen; he takes up boxing.
1960	• Cassius Clay wins the Olympic Gold Medal and his first professional fight.
1964	• Beats Sonny Liston, becomes heavyweight champ and renounces his name, becoming Muhammad Ali.
1967	• Refuses induction into U.S. Army and is stripped of boxing license.
1970	• Ali is allowed to box again.
1971	• Ali-Frazier I, The Fight.
1974	• Ali-Frazier II; Ali-Foreman, the Rumble in the Jungle; Muhammad Ali meets Veronica Porche.
1975	• Ali-Frazier III, the Thrilla in Manila.
1977	• December 30, Laila Ali is born in Miami, Florida.
1980	• Muhammad Ali is knocked out by Larry Holmes.
1981	• Muhammad Ali boxes his last fight, versus Trevor Berbick.
1996	• Muhammad Ali lights Olympic torch, Atlanta.
1999	• Laila Ali's first professional fight, versus April Fowler.
2000	• Muhammad Ali is named a United Nations Messenger of Peace.
2002	• Laila Ali becomes super-middleweight champion (IBA, WIBA, IWBF).
2003	• Laila Ali knocks out Christy Martin.
2005	• Muhammad Ali Center for the Advancement of Humanity to open.

# BOXING RECORDS

Selected Boxing Record of Muhammad Ali

W won
L lost
KO knockout
TKO technical knockout (bout stopped by referee)
(Numerals following above abbreviations refer to round number)
WORLD world championship bout

1960
- October 29, Tunney Hunsaker, Louisville, Kentucky, W6
- December 27, Herb Siler, Miami Beach, Florida, KO4

1961
- January 17, Anthony Sperti, Miami Beach, Florida, KO3
- February 7, Jim Robinson, Miami Beach, Florida, KO1
- February 21, Donnie Fleeman, Miami Beach, Florida, KO7
- April 19, Lamar Clark, Louisville, Kentucky, KO2
- June 26, Duke Sabedong, Las Vegas, Nevada, W10
- July 22, Alonzo Johnson, Louisville, Kentucky, W10
- October 7, Alex Miteff, Louisville, Kentucky, KO6
- November 29, Willie Besmanoff, Louisville, Kentucky, KO7

1962
- February 10, Sonny Banks, New York, New York, KO4
- February 28, Don Warner, Miami Beach, Florida KO4
- April 23, George Logan, Los Angeles, California, KO6
- May 19, Billy Daniels, New York, New York, KO7
- July 20, Alejandro Lavorante, Los Angeles, California, KO5
- November 15, Archie Moore, Los Angeles, California, KO4

1963
- January 24, Charlie Powell, Pittsburgh, Pennsylvania, KO3
- March 13, Doug Jones, New York, New York, W10
- June 18, Henry Cooper, London, England, KO5

1964
- February 25, Sonny Liston, Miami Beach, Florida, TKO7, WORLD

1965
- May 25, Sonny Liston, Lewiston, Maine, KO1, WORLD
- November 22, Floyd Patterson, Las Vegas, Nevada, KO12, WORLD

1966
- March 29, George Chuvalo, Toronto, Canada, W15, WORLD
- May 21, Henry Cooper, London, England, KO6, WORLD
- August 6, Brian London, London, England, KO3, WORLD
- September 10, Karl Mildenberger, Frankfurt, Germany, KO12, WORLD

1966	• November 14, Cleveland Williams, Houston, Texas, KO3, WORLD
1967	• February 6, Ernie Terrell, Houston, Texas, W15, WORLD
	• March 22, Zora Folley, New York, New York, KO7, WORLD
1970	• October 26, Jerry Quarry, Atlanta, Georgia, KO3
	• December 7, Oscar Bonavena, New York, New York, KO15
1971	• March 8, Joe Frazier, New York, New York, L15, WORLD
	• July 26, Jimmy Ellis, Houston, Texas, KO12
	• November 17, Buster Mathis, Houston, Texas, W12
	• December 26, Jurgen Blin, Zurich, Switzerland, KO7
1972	• April 1, Mac Foster, Tokyo, Japan, W15
	• May 1, George Chuvalo, Vancouver, Canada, W12
	• June 27, Jerry Quarry, Las Vegas, Nevada, KO7
	• July 19, Alvin Lewis, Dublin, Ireland, KO11
	• September 20, Floyd Patterson, New York, New York, KO8
	• November 21, Bob Foster, Stateline, Nevada KO8
1973	• February 14, Joe Bugner, Las Vegas, Nevada, W12
	• March 31, Ken Norton, San Diego, California, L12
	• September 10, Ken Norton, Los Angeles, California, W12
	• October 20, Rudy Lubbers, Jakarta, Indonesia, W12
1974	• January 28, Joe Frazier, New York, New York, W12
	• October 30, George Foreman, Kinshasa, Zaire, KO8, WORLD
1975	• March 24, Chuck Wepner, Cleveland, Ohio, KO15, WORLD
	• May 16, Ron Lyle, Las Vegas, Nevada, KO11, WORLD
	• June 30, Joe Bugner, Kuala Lumpur, Malaysia, W15, WORLD
	• October 1, Joe Frazier, Quezon City, Philippines, KO14, WORLD
1976	• February 20, Jean-Pierre Coopman, Hato Rey, Puerto Rico, KO5, WORLD
	• April 30, Jimmy Young, Landover, Maryland, W15, WORLD
	• May 24, Richard Dunn, Munich, Germany, KO5, WORLD
	• September 28, Ken Norton, New York, New York, W15, WORLD
1977	• May 16, Alfredo Evangelista, Landover, Maryland, W15, WORLD
	• September 29, Earnie Shavers, New York, New York, W15, WORLD
1978	• February 15, Leon Spinks, Las Vegas, Nevada, L15, WORLD
	• September 15, Leon Spinks, New Orleans, Louisiana, W15, WORLD
1980	• October 2, Larry Holmes, Las Vegas, Nevada, KO11, WORLD
1981	• December 11, Trevor Berbick, Nassau, Bahamas, L10

 # BOXING RECORDS

Laila Ali Career Record

1999
- October 8, April Fowler, Verona, New York, KO1
- November 10, Shadina Pennybaker, Chester, West Virginia, TKO4
- December 10, Nicolyn Armstrong, Detroit, Michigan, TKO2

2000
- March 7, Crystal Arcand, Windsor, Ontario, Canada, KO1
- April 8, Karen Bill, Detroit, Michigan, TKO3
- April 22, Kristina King, Guangzhou, China, TKO 4
- June 15, Marjorie Jones, Hollywood, California, TKO 1
- October 20, Kendra Lenhart, Auburn Hills, Michigan, W6

2001
- March 2, Christine Robinson, Verona, New York, TKO5
- June 8, Jacquiline Frazier-Lyde, Verona, New York, W8

2002
- June 7, Shirvelle Williams, Southaven, Mississippi, W6
- August 17, Suzette Taylor, Las Vegas, Nevada, TKO 2 (for WIBA Super Middleweight title)
- November 8, Valerie Mahfoud, Las Vegas, Nevada, TKO 8 (for WIBA, IWBF, IBA Super Middleweight title)

2003
- February 14, Mary Ann Almager, Louisville, Kentucky, TKO4
- June 21, Valerie Mahfoud, Los Angeles, California, TKO 6
- August 23, Christy Martin, Biloxi, Mississippi, KO4

2004
- July 17, Nikki Epilan, Bowie, Maryland, KTO4
- July 30, Monica Nunez, Louisville, Kentucky, TK09

belt An ornamental belt awarded to a champion in a weight division. The belt also refers to the championship itself.

cornermen A fighter's training and support team (trainer and doctor, typically), so named because they stand in the fighter's corner, just outside the ring.

decision A fight in which no knockout or disqualification occurs is won by decision, meaning the judges add up the points scored by each fighter. The win can come by unanimous decision (all judges agree) or by split decision (one judge scores fighter A as having won, the other two score fighter B as the winner).

disqualification A referee can disqualify a fighter for repeatedly breaking the rules (for example, hitting below the belt—roughly the waistline—of the opposing fighter). Typically, the referee cautions the offending fighter a set number of times. If the fighter continues with illegal blows or activity, the referee can disqualify him or her.

draw A fight in which the boxers are tied on points on the score-cards kept by the judges. Neither boxer wins.

knockout (KO) A fighter is knocked out, and loses the fight, if the opponent hits him or her so hard that he or she is knocked down and stays on the canvas for ten seconds.

main event The headline bout on a fight card. Preliminary bouts are collectively known as the undercard.

Nation of Islam Also known as the Black Muslim movement, it is a spiritual and political black supremacist movement.

referee An official who stands in the ring with the fighters, watches for illegal blows, and sometimes separates the fighters.

ring The square area in which a boxing match takes place. The floor of the ring is called the canvas, and the ring is surrounded by ropes.

scorecards A running count of points kept by the judges. The scorecards decide the winner of a fight if no knockout or disqualification occurs.

technical knockout (TKO) This occurs when a fighter is repeatedly knocked down, or if the referee believes he or she cannot or should not continue to box. If a fighter quits fighting, or if his or her corner throws in the towel (an accepted sign of surrender), the fighter is also considered to have lost by TKO.

title defense A boxing champion in a given weight division (such as featherweight or heavyweight) who holds that division's title is required to defend his or her title against challenges from other boxers.

venue A place for large gatherings, such as a sports stadium or boxing arena.

Web Sites

Due to the changing nature of Internet links, the Rosen Publishing Group, Inc., has developed an online list of Web sites related to the subject of this book. This site is updated regularly. Please use this link to access the list.

http://www.rosenlinks.com/fafa/mala

Ali, Laila, with Ritz, David. *Reach!: Finding Strength, Spirit, and Personal Power.* New York: Hyperion, 2002.

Atyea, Don. *Muhammad Ali:The Glory Years.* Los Angeles: Miramax, 2003.

Beard, Ben. *Muhammad Ali: The Greatest.* Winterville, GA: June Bug Books, 2002.

Dyson, Cindy. *Laila Ali.* New York: Chelsea House, 2001.

Latimer, Clay. *Muhammad Ali (Journey to Freedom).* Chanhassen, MN: Child's World, 2000.

Myers, Walter Dean. *The Greatest: Muhammad Ali.* New York: Scholastic Signature, 2003.

Remnick, David. *King of the World: Muhammad Ali and the Rise of an American Hero.* New York: Vintage Books, 1999.

★★★ BIBLIOGRAPHY

Ali, Laila, with David Ritz. *Reach*. New York: Hyperion, 2002.

Askmen.com. "Laila Ali: Why We Like Her." Retrieved February 5, 2004 (http://www.askmen.com/women/ models_200/202_laila_ali.html).

Costas, Bob. "Costas on Ali," *Rolling Stone*, May 15, 2003, p. 116.

Dunn, Katherine, "One Ring Circus," *Sports Illustrated Women*, September 2001, p. 82.

Hauser, Thomas. *Muhammad Ali: His Life and Times*. New York: Simon & Schuster, 1989.

Kram, Mark. *Ghosts of Manila*. New York: HarperCollins, 2001.

"Laila Ali." *Newsmakers*, Issue 2. Gale Group, 2001.

Laila Ali Official Web Site. Laila Ali bio. Retrieved January 7, 2004 (http://www.lailaali.net).

Lipsyte, Robert. *Free to Be Muhammad Ali*. New York: Harper & Row, 1978.

"Muhammad Ali." *Newsmakers* 1997, Issue 4. Gale Research, 1997.

Myers, Walter Dean. *The Greatest*. New York: Scholastic Press, 2001.

Remnick, David. *King of the World*. New York: Random House, 1998.

Smith, Timothy W. "Another Ali Enters the Ring: His Daughter." *New York Times*, February 23, 1999.

Weinman, Sam, "Ali Has Slowed, but Still Packs Punch," *Journal News*, February 26, 2004. Retrieved February 10, 2004 (http://www.thejournalnews.com/newsroom/020604/c0106alico.html)

Willis, George, "A Couple of Champs—Nothing's Impossible for Ali, Daughter," *New York Post*, February 6, 2004, p. 112.

Wood, Daniel B. "Muhammad Ali Takes on New Opponent: Intolerance," *Christian Science Monitor*, December 5, 1996, p. 3.

INDEX

About the Author

Tim Ungs lives on a farm in central Kentucky with his wife and family.

4/13

DOGS SET X

BULL TERRIERS

Tamara L. Britton
ABDO Publishing Company

visit us at
www.abdopublishing.com

Published by ABDO Publishing Company, PO Box 398166, Minneapolis, MN 55439.
Copyright © 2013 by Abdo Consulting Group, Inc. International copyrights reserved
in all countries. No part of this book may be reproduced in any form without written
permission from the publisher. The Checkerboard Library™ is a trademark and logo of
ABDO Publishing Company.

Printed in the United States of America, North Mankato, Minnesota.
102012
012013

 PRINTED ON RECYCLED PAPER

Cover Photo: SuperStock
Interior Photos: Alamy pp. 5, 19, 21; AP Images pp. 7, 12, 13; iStockphoto pp. 8, 9, 10,
        11, 17; Thinkstock p. 15

Editors: Megan M. Gunderson, Stephanie Hedlund
Art Direction: Neil Klinepier

Cataloging-in-Publication Data

Britton, Tamara L., 1963-
  Bull terriers / Tamara L. Britton.
     p. cm. -- (Dogs)
  Includes bibliographical references and index.
  ISBN 978-1-61783-589-6
  1. Bull terrier--Juvenile literature. 2. Dogs--Juvenile literature. I. Title.
  636.7/55--dc23
                      2012946333

CONTENTS

THE DOG FAMILY

Americans own more than 78 million dogs! All of these dogs are members of the family **Canidae**. The name comes from the Latin word for "dog," which is *canis*.

For more than 12,000 years, dogs and humans have lived and worked together. Early humans were hunters. They adopted wolf pups to help them hunt. Modern dogs descended from these early wolf pups.

Eventually, humans settled into farming communities. They developed different dog **breeds** to assist in new tasks. Hunting and guarding breeds protected farmers' flocks. Terriers kept stored grains free of **rodents**.

But not everyone needed a working dog. Some people just wanted a companion dog. So, **breeders** began to develop dogs to be companions. One of these breeds was the playful bull terrier.

The bull terrier

BULL TERRIERS

By the early 1800s, **breeders** had developed the bull-and-terrier. These dogs were a mix of a bulldog and a terrier. They participated in the sport of **bullbaiting**.

In the 1860s, James Hinks of Birmingham, England, wanted to create a companion animal from this fighting breed. He crossed the bull-and-terrier with the dalmatian, the bulldog, and the white English terrier. In this way, Hinks created the bull terrier.

Bull terriers proved to be good companion dogs. Their popularity soon spread beyond England. The **American Kennel Club (AKC)** recognized the bull terrier in 1885. Then in 1897, the Bull Terrier Club of America was established.

Today, everyone recognizes the bull terrier! It is the AKC's fifty-first most popular breed.

WHAT THEY'RE LIKE

The bull terrier's muscular build and stern expression can make it seem unfriendly. But, nothing could be further from the truth! These active dogs are sweet and fun-loving.

Bullies are lively and playful. They love to stay busy and should have toys to keep them occupied. Otherwise they will occupy themselves with your possessions!

Bull terriers are known as the clowns of the dog world.

What is your bully saying to you?

These affectionate dogs are very devoted to family. If kept apart, they are not happy. Bullies love to be close to their people. They will even go so far as to sit on them!

Bullies will sometimes "talk" with groans and grunts. However, they do not bark very often. If your bully is barking, you'll want to find out why!

Coat and Color

The bull terrier has a short, flat, glossy coat. Your bull terrier may **shed** its coat, especially in the spring and autumn. Frequent brushing will help keep fur off your couch! Other than this, the bull terrier needs little grooming.

The bull terrier's coat comes in two varieties. They are white and colored. White bullies can have a spot of color on their heads. But their bodies are all white.

A white bull terrier

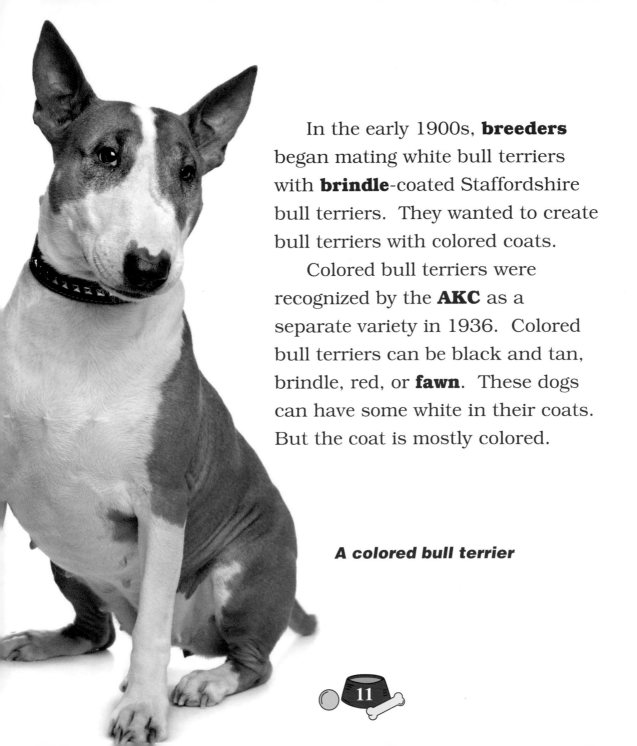

In the early 1900s, **breeders** began mating white bull terriers with **brindle**-coated Staffordshire bull terriers. They wanted to create bull terriers with colored coats.

Colored bull terriers were recognized by the **AKC** as a separate variety in 1936. Colored bull terriers can be black and tan, brindle, red, or **fawn**. These dogs can have some white in their coats. But the coat is mostly colored.

A colored bull terrier

SIZE

Bull terriers are strong, sturdy dogs. Males are 20 to 24 inches (51 to 61 cm) tall. They weigh 50 to 80 pounds (23 to 36 kg). Female bullies are slightly smaller.

The bully's short, strong body has a broad chest. A long, thick neck holds a distinctive egg-shaped head. A long, blunt snout is sided by small,

Rufus is a colored male bull terrier. His egg-shaped head is perfect.

Violet is a white female bull terrier. She has nice triangle-shaped eyes.

triangle-shaped eyes. It is tipped with a black nose. Small, pointed ears perch close together on top of the head.

This stout body sits on straight, medium-length legs that end in small, round feet. A thin tail is thicker at the dog's rear end and tapers to a sharp point.

CARE

All dogs need regular visits to the veterinarian for checkups. The veterinarian will give them **vaccines** against common diseases. He or she can also **spay** or **neuter** your bully.

Bull terriers can develop several health problems. Kidney, heart, and skin problems are common in this **breed**. The veterinarian can watch for these issues and work to keep your dog healthy.

It is important to keep your bully's teeth clean. Brush its teeth every day with toothpaste made just for dogs. You can use this time to check your

Though its short coat is easy to care for, an active bully may need an occasional bath!

bully's eyes, ears, and feet. And don't forget to trim its nails!

Regular exercise is also important. Bullies love games and outdoor activities! So, spend some time playing with your dog every day.

FEEDING

All dogs have their own dietary needs. These depend on several factors such as age, size, and level of exercise. Your veterinarian can suggest a diet based on your dog's lifestyle.

Bully owners should provide their dogs with a healthy diet. Puppies need several small meals a day. Older dogs can eat one meal each day. All bullies need plenty of fresh water. Be sure to change the water every day!

It is easy for dogs to gain weight. Excess weight stresses joints. It can lead to heart and kidney disease, **diabetes**, and a shorter life span. So, carefully watch the amount of food your bully eats.

An active bull terrier can easily maintain a healthy weight.

THINGS THEY NEED

Bull terriers are active and lively! So, owners must make time for their dogs. Daily walks are important. Toys can help provide exercise, too.

Every bully needs a collar with license and identification tags. A **microchip** can also keep your bully safe.

At home, a crate offers your bully a quiet place to rest. It can also help with housebreaking puppies. Large, sturdy food and water bowls are a must.

These material things are important. But most of all, a dog needs a loving family, **socialization**, and training. This will result in a well-behaved dog.

Walking your bully will give it the physical and mental stimulation it needs.

PUPPIES

A bull terrier mother is **pregnant** for about 63 days. Then, she gives birth to a **litter** of puppies. Five puppies is the average litter size for a bull terrier.

The newborn puppies are blind and deaf. They can see and hear after 2 weeks. At 3 weeks, the puppies begin taking their first steps. At 12 weeks old, bully puppies are ready for a loving home.

Have you decided the bull terrier is the right **breed** for your family? If so, it's time to find a reputable breeder! This is important because good breeders only work with healthy dogs. They test parent dogs for health problems before breeding them.

Be prepared to answer many questions about your lifestyle. Good breeders care about their dogs and puppies for the whole of their lives. They want their puppies to go to good homes.

When you get your puppy home, begin basic obedience training as soon as it is settled. Bullies will bond with their owners as they train together. A well cared for bull terrier will be a loving family companion for 10 to 12 years.

Bullies love attention, so they will love training! Be sure to reward good performance with praise, treats, and lots of love.

GLOSSARY

American Kennel Club (AKC) - an organization that studies and promotes interest in purebred dogs.

breed - a group of animals sharing the same ancestors and appearance. A breeder is a person who raises animals. Raising animals is often called breeding them.

brindle - having dark streaks or spots on a gray, tan, or tawny background.

bullbaiting - a former sport in which dogs fought with bulls.

Canidae (KAN-uh-dee) - the scientific Latin name for the dog family. Members of this family are called canids. They include wolves, jackals, foxes, coyotes, and domestic dogs.

diabetes - a disease in which the body cannot properly absorb normal amounts of sugar and starch.

fawn - a light grayish brown color.

litter - all of the puppies born at one time to a mother dog.

microchip - an electronic circuit placed under an animal's skin. A microchip contains identifying information that can be read by a scanner.

neuter (NOO-tuhr) - to remove a male animal's reproductive glands.

pregnant - having one or more babies growing within the body.

rodent - any of several related animals that have large front teeth for gnawing. Common rodents include mice, squirrels, and beavers.

shed - to cast off hair, feathers, skin, or other coverings or parts by a natural process.

socialize - to adapt an animal to behaving properly around people or other animals in various settings.

spay - to remove a female animal's reproductive organs.

vaccine (vak-SEEN) - a shot given to prevent illness or disease.

WEB SITES

To learn more about bull terriers, visit ABDO Publishing Company online. Web sites about bull terriers are featured on our Book Links page. These links are routinely monitored and updated to provide the most current information available.

www.abdopublishing.com

INDEX